SONGENIZIOS

SONGENIZIOS

poems

Michael Garrigan   Andrew Jones

COMPETENT
BACKSTOP

Cover design and layout: Andrew Jones
First Edition, June 2020

ISBN: 9798652698072

Competent Backstop Press
Dubuque, Iowa

All proceeds from the sale of this chapbook are being donated to the Sweet Relief Musicians Fund to support members of the music industry.

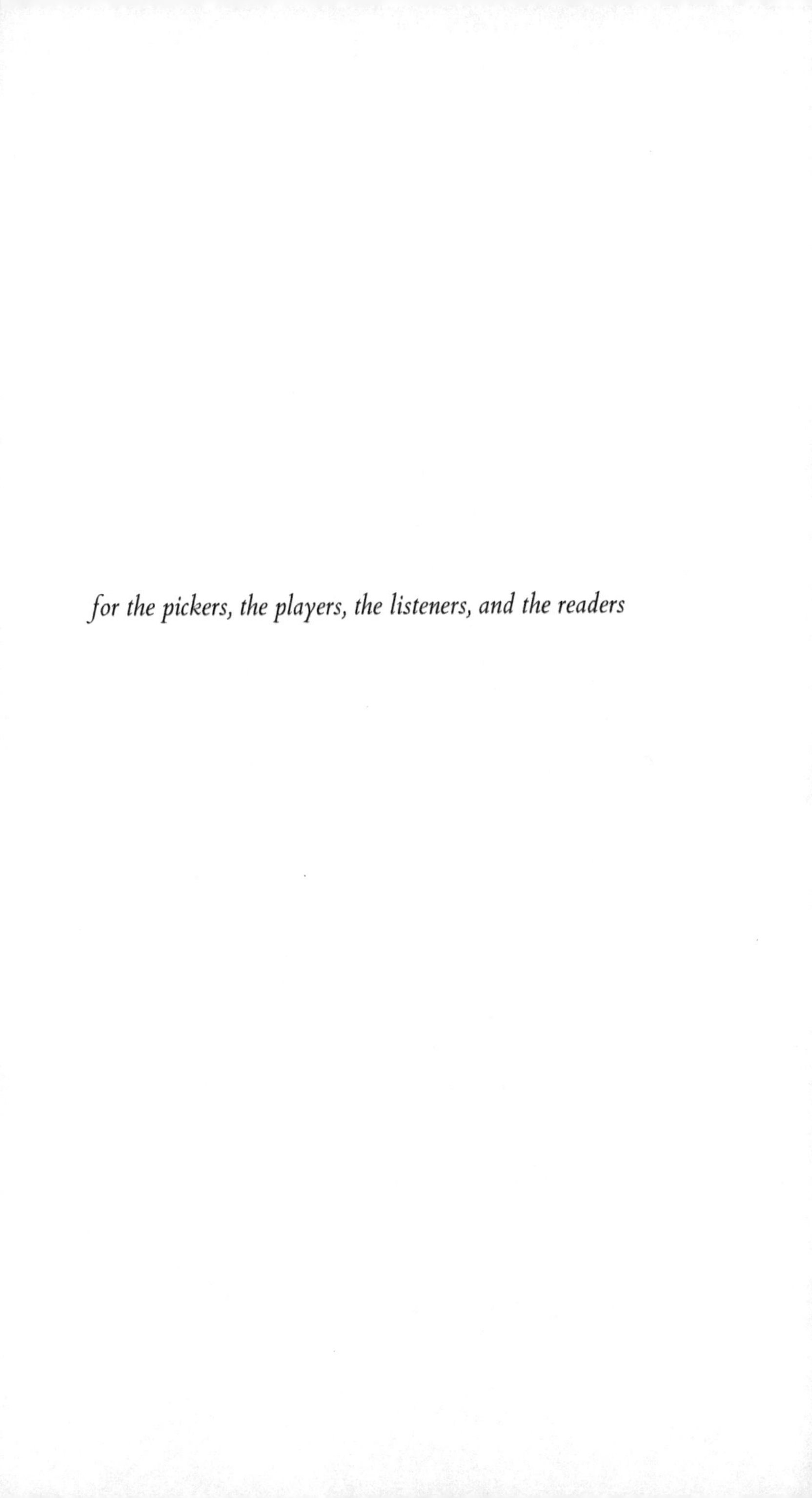

for the pickers, the players, the listeners, and the readers

CONTENTS

Wanted: Mix Tape Collaborator
An Introduction

> *Such a delicious pain in the ass to make,*
> *on a double deck if you were lucky,*
> —Brenda Shaughnessy, "A Mix Tape:
> 'Don't You Forget About Me'"

Maybe it's the way a song lyric can channel your internal monologue. Or an appreciation for a stranger's selection bursting from the jukebox in some basement dive bar. Or a mix tape found in a faux-wood cassette box at a yard sale. Maybe it's most like jamming in a garage with the bass player who responded to the photocopied flyer you posted on the bulletin board at the local record store.

I love invented forms and collaboration, so when I first encountered Kim Addonizio's "Sonnenizio on a Line from Drayton," I was instantly smitten. Take a line from an existing sonnet, use it as the opening line for a new sonnet, repeat one word (in some form) from that first line in all the following lines, and then end with a rhyming couplet. There exists in this creation: something formal, but not too formal, and a dialogue with another work of poetry or a poet. The form functions as a challenge and the outcome hinges on the selection of one little word.

The kernel of an idea for this collaboration began in a passenger van loaded with Nature Writing students on a highway near Abiquiú, New Mexico in the spring of 2019. I was trying to formulate a writing plan for myself, separate from the coursework my students would undertake, during our stay at Ghost Ranch. I slipped buds into my ears and pressed play on Scott Hirsch's album, *Lost Time Behind the Moon.* "I'm a purple diamond at the break of day." The lyric stuck with me and I used it to write a sonnenizio the next morning. But then...no more. Other ideas came and filled my stay.

Fast forward to social-distancing in the spring of 2020. A cold morning in my basement, I put on Hirsch again and the same lyric pulled me back to the sonnenizio idea. I knew I would fail again without accountability—it was too easy to let nearly everything slide at the moment. I needed a collaborator. Enter Michael Garrigan. Our writing has been published in the same journals a few times and the chain of follows on social media put us in each other's feeds. So I sent along my crazy idea: make a mix tape/playlist of a dozen songs, pass it on to the other person, and begin writing sonnenizios inspired by and using a line from the songs we received. He agreed. Within a week, we had playlists from one another. Within a month, we had enough for this chapbook and a new name for the form: the songenizio.

AJ

Making mix tapes and playlists is a kind of metaphysical act for me. The pressing of the play and record button down at the same time, the click of the reels, the hiss of the tape, the sharing of a link, the finding of the perfect opening and closing songs, the tracking, the cover art, the mystery of just how this music will be received—it creates an ethereal bond between the artist and the listener and the giver and the receiver. A communion. A faith in Side B. When Andrew reached out with his songenizio idea, I jumped at the chance to create a playlist for someone I had never met (what better way to introduce yourself?) and to discover new music. I've never really enjoyed writing formal poetry. I'm much more of a rambler. My poems take the shape of the rivers I wade, so I was a bit apprehensive about writing in a set form, but I went with it anyway, the excitement of sharing songs just too hard to pass up.

Sharing music has always been a way for me to share stories and experiences. Here, check this Cass McCombs track out, maybe that melody will catch you like it did me as a bat careened across a full moon silhouetting a dying campfire. Maybe you can feel that smoke smoldering in those Steve Gunn guitar licks. Maybe you can smell the honeysuckle along the river lifting that Woods chorus into a holy mantra.

The quarantine, which had just started when Andrew reached out, magnified the power of formal poetry and the experience of sharing music. All of a sudden, I lost almost all human interaction and the energy that I fed off of and my days lost their structure. It was my daily bike ride along the river and listening to Andrew's playlist that gave me something to hold onto during those early days of the pandemic. It became a way of communicating with someone through song. Each one was a little piece of kindling we handed each other, waiting to see what kind of fire the other would create in their own isolation. A conversation centered on music and poetry. What a beautiful thing. Writing these poems in this form gave me a structure I needed during a time when all the structures I knew were disintegrating. Music and poetry have the power to give us something we never knew we needed.

MG
June 2020

PROGRAM
1

On a Line from Mount Moriah
"Eureka Springs"

We waded into the healing spring
waiting for a bottomless bright morning
light to bring a balm for last night's tired miles,
our bodies become tongues, sulphur and salt,
wanting more than this torched life on the trail,
yearning for a baptism from a stone seap,
for a cleansing of our toiled chapped lips and
our sweat-stained blacktopped t-shirts strung across
our bodies weighted to river's slow wake
behind concrete contours of the Hoover
Dam. A stoup hidden up a steep ravine
that if approached right, offers atonement.
Wading into the healing spring we stripped,
into absolved totems as water dripped.

MG

On a Line from Smog

"Running the Loping"

I lay on the bed in the dark, laughing,
emjambed at day's end, bathed in bonfire
smoke. Bedsprings creak softer than the owl's call.
Strange bedfellows: my joy and death's emblem.
Blame the moon's distorted albedo, blame
the bedsheet's pull. Call it an embrace
of bedlam, an internal dialogue.
But this is no deathbed evening. No one's
succumbed to despair. We aren't alone
in this bedarkening, despite such a
bedraggled appearance. The breeze shivers
my bed, rustles pages. A scarf of clouds,
like a streambed, slides past my windows.
Bedeviled by strange hope, my laughter grows.

AJ

On a Line from Marie/Lepanto
"The Rail"

quietness, wilderness, the devil's breath
across a wild manzanita palm
leaves of green, bark of red, a wildness
in the elbow, a quick bewilderment
that lands in a wild riffle ravine,
diaphanous sea of wildflowers
bathing in a wildfire streaking
wildly across the night before snow
bewildered our saddle of Devil's peaks.
We woke to white. We became wildebeests,
Feral, wilding our teeth into
pebbles, our eyes into wildered pitch.
Quietness bewilders our insides,
wildness in each breath that never dies.

MG

On a Line from Cass McCombs
"Rounder"

On slick embers going past the gamblers
we called brazen bluff a go-between,
an ongoing attempt to craft losses
into an archipelago of life.
We were moviegoers in the gloaming:
always on some edge, egotistical
lovers foregoing the debt of success.
A roll of the dice to negotiate;
the river card against an embargo.
We called it a fandango, sang along
to "Scarlet Begonias" over blacktop
miles, and carried little in cargo.
A largo-tempo life was our one bet—
a go-to ante we haven't lost yet.

AJ

PROGRAM
2

On a Line from Trampled by Turtles
"Victory"

Borrowed from nothing, come back half alive,
shared syllables are incoming handshakes,
songs for a homecoming drawn out from some
distant source. You become a spliced reel
of images: the newcomer's themes
triggering your unwelcome memories.
Clutch tight the comeuppance, self-directed
as it might be. Ghosts cometh, says the poet,
and you inhale her comely words.
The reward is the outcome of moving
nouns, near rhymes coming from lyrics.
Poems are always forthcoming, shrouded
latecomers longing for the slowest dance,
a comeback waiting for half a chance.

AJ

On a Line from John Moreland
"It Don't Suit Me (Like Before)"

We sit comparing scars, strumming on the stars
that once were dust under our dirty feet
waiting for one of us to claim victory.
Conversations under moonlight always
seem to fade, blinking lightning bug notions,
like two bird dogs we point at darkness, one
rustle and we're off, nettles on our skin,
burns soaked with whiskey, fire, Dylan concerts
on cassettes, lonesome pedal steel blinds us
into early morning light. We once walked
home from high school through abandoned quarries
thinking we'd share a longer freedom than
that short strap frontier. All that's left—some wood,
starched deer bones, and Wilco's "Misunderstood."

MG

On a Line from Woods
"With Light and with Love"

A hell by its own, still I hold you dear—
holdout among dissolving years. This song,
like a chokehold, like an old negative,
calling you back: was it as shareholder?
or just as placeholder before crossing
thresholds, true directions forward, terrain.
You dangled toes in the stream, withholding
purposes, just a fingerhold on desire—
honesty never your calling, footholds
never sturdy. But hold up! You forced
us all to chart fresh courses, holding fast
catalysts meant to craft our households
into freeholds. Lyric: jar us, stir those
memories, souvenirs held in repose.

AJ

On a Line from Arbouretum
"Oceans Don't Sing"

Statements and plans that were made, passing by
as we drive, stateless, borderless, homeless
up and down this Pacific cradled state,
we fall into ditch kingdoms. Apostates
we have become, thieving wild estates
as we traverse interstates slicing through
fault lines, wineries, and understated
smog sunsets. We devastate the inside
of our old forms, a new state of being
that gestates in our beards and granola.
Statements scratched across sand, silent prayers to
Joshua Tree crucifixions substates
of full moon oceans. Here is our new state,
a statement of calling, a song of fate.

MG

PROGRAM
3

On a Line from Magnolia Electric Co.
"Song for Willie"

For one the western skies and for the rest—
just a thermarest and the ground we found
tonight as we barreled through thick forests
along the Klamath until, resting, sand
and ocean and a footrest of driftwood.
We fall after three beers as the waves crest
into a sleep that rustles, that wrestles
itself under thin nylon tents, a rest
that lays heavy in dreams of spruce forests,
elk, seal, quail, trestles of a wilderness,
a Lost Coast catachrestic landscape.
Let us rest easy in this collision
of cresting water and eroding rock
and this is all that the rest of us hold,
redwoods to rest eyes on a river fold.

MG

On a Line from Scott Hirsch
"No No"

Back to California, where the grass grows
into waves of pilsner, where you switchback
hills littered with hunchbacked oaks, run wild
by lean coyotes. Your voice backscatters:
soft lyrics spoken backwards, intentions
called back from lost flyover country years.
Backslider, you hum in the dry air, like
feedback lifting the hair on her neck.
Back to California, where refuge waits,
where fiddleback music pulls you under
the groove. The fog enters on a backdraft,
draws back like a timid lover waiting.
The sun falls at your backdoor, a golden
backsplash covering you 'til dawn rolls in.

AJ

On a Line from Hiss Golden Messenger
"Westering"

Now do you heed how his voice does ring?
It speaks of downtown, it speaks of barrooms,
it whispers through concrete kaleidoscopic
watersheds, it sings three rivers done got
us down deep in these blues, down deep in these
ravines where city lights fade and we doze
in a ghost river, city shadows creep
through single speed wheel spokes, we holdout hand
rolled cigarettes, smoke curls hazardous
hands, trains tornado by, we pound pavement
see city blurring into abandoned
dreams, its voices crescendoing chorus
of the wisdom we seek, of the freedom
to shakedown into new mycelium.

MG

On a Line from The Dead Tongues
"Ebb and Flow"

Silhouettes of the weeping willow trees
followed you between grave sites, over
the fallow earth around ancient markers
as you lowered the scrub brush to granite
forcing away the yellow moss and dirt
to reveal my ancestral names below.
Swallows darted from lake edge to gravel
in the mellow Wisconsin afternoon—
fellow explorers of the map of the dead.
One name in lowercase letters, comes clear
as the shallow request legend tells us
she made: "bury me not with low Germans
who fill this land." Yet, you, my low-key wife,
a Heinz at birth, slowly bring her name to life.

AJ

PROGRAM
4

On a Line from Courtney Barnett
"Help Your Self"

Darkness depends on where you're standing,
a simple bystander in this Iowa
barn with straw bales for a grandstand,
the singer asking you to withstand a bit
of heartbreak, the steel player in a standoff
with the keys, while kids practice handstands
on the lawn under fireflies on standby,
waiting to flare, to break the dark standstill
of surrounding corn. Stand back on your heels
like a kickstand, bob your head, let that grin
slip out. Nothing about this is standard.
Understand this as akin to worship,
all of us standing close, music as tether.
Understand we fill the darkness together.

AJ

On a Line from Joan Shelley
"Teal"

Shock of teal blue clouds gathering in light
as we watch taillights of another truck
coursing its way through moonlight and mayflies.
Here, the river is light enough to hold,
so we hold it, searchlights between fingers,
brook trout halos lighting blue, red pebbles
into a vermiculating flight, a
slight mirroring so sky, river, moon, we
melt into a delight that casts across
the ethereal twilight between skin
of stonefly husk, human, hickory. Blight
has reached the Ash, they are dying. Unlike
these trout, they feel no plight of man, no they
hold clouds and light together as we pray.

MG

On a Line from Steve Gunn

"Ancient Jules"

Far from the world was the mystic fool,
farming stanzas, hybrid syntax, and songs.
He christened it a farrago of life,
a farcical poetics meant to save
himself from farsightedness, from despair
and its dark safari of loneliness.
During bleak Fargo winter, he warmed bones
under the moon, believed the farside might
be littered with fertile farmland: so rich
with farfetched sounds he hadn't yet heard.
Come spring, he won at faro with the dawn,
and planted his cards—little farthings of hope—
to grow beside the farmhouse. In his car,
he journeyed on, to spread his word afar.

AJ

On a Line from Beulah
"Sunday Under Glass"

Slow prayers with no answers must go somewhere
even in a sky devoid of gods we
have rivers that listen, allegories
and metaphors negotiate another
liturgy. It was slow with an ego
that filled this valley to write a gospel
worthy enough to sing, full of goodness.
But now that we have one we gorge on its
melody, throats full of chords, forgotten
notes behind our knees, goldfinches eddy
in the slow crescendo, even maggots
find an instrument to play. Let us go
somewhere gorgeous, a landscape made of song,
gone to where we should have been all along.

MG

ACKNOWLEDGMENTS

Grateful acknowledgment is made to the artists whose songs inspired these poems:

Mount Moriah. "Eureka Springs." *Miracle Temple,* Merge Records, 2013.
Smog. "Running the Loping." *A River Ain't Too Much to Love,* Drag City, 2005.
Marie/Lepanto. "The Rail." *Tenkiller,* Big Legal Mess Records, 2018.
Cass McCombs. "Rounder." *Tip of the Sphere,* Anti-, 2019.
Trampled by Turtles. "Victory." *Palomino,* Banjodad Records, 2010.
John Moreland. "It Don't Suit Me (Like Before)." *Big Bad Luv,* 4AD, 2017.
Woods. "With Light and with Love." *With Light and with Love,* Woodsist, 2014.
Arbouretum. "Oceans Don't Sing." *Coming Out of the Fog,* Thrill Jockey, 2013.
Magnolia Electric Co. "Song for Willie." *Josephine,* Secretly Canadian, 2009.
Scott Hirsch. "No No." *Lost Time Behind the Moon,* Scissor Tail, 2018.
Hiss Golden Messenger. "Westering." *Poor Moon,* Paradise of Bachelors, 2012.
The Dead Tongues. "Ebb and Flow." *Unsung Passage,* Psychic Hotline, 2018.
Courtney Barnett. "Help Your Self." *Tell Me How You Really Feel,* Mom + Pop, Milk! Records, 2018.
Joan Shelley. "Teal." *Like the River Loves the Sea,* No Quarter, 2019.
Steve Gunn. "Ancient Jules." *Eyes on the Lines,* Matador, 2016.
Beulah. "Sunday Under Glass." *When Your Heartstrings Break,* Sugar Free Records, 1999.